Big Bear, Little Bear and Dementia

Lovingly written by Katie Faulkner
Beautifully illustrated by Iain Welch

Hello, it's lovely to meet you.

Hello, my name is Katie. I'd like to thank you for taking the time to read this. I'd like to start off by recognising that if you are here, there is a chance that you are going through a difficult time in your life. I hope that you are able to be as kind to yourself as you are to the people you love.

If you are reading because you want to see the creation of truly dementia friendly generations - thank you. At the time of writing this, over 850,000 people in the UK are living with dementia, so it is ever more important to challenge the perceived societal norms of what it means to live with dementia whilst supporting each other with understanding, love and empathy. Just know that whatever your reason, I am grateful that you are taking the time to read this book.

Our brains control everything we think, say and do. They also store our loves, laughs and memories. When a person is living with dementia, they are no longer always in control of these things. This can be a complex situation to navigate, especially for the person affected and their loved ones.

My first encounter with dementia was with my Great Gran. She was the lady who always knew the answer. She knew how to make me laugh and how to make me feel better. Then all of a sudden, she didn't. My family were ever so supportive and did their best to explain why Gran had suddenly changed, but as a child I did not understand and felt hurt when my Gran no longer recognised me. I am certain this resonates with so many little bears who are living a similar story.

This experience no doubt lead me towards becoming a physiotherapist specialising in supporting people living with dementia. I have had the privilege of spending time with many wonderful people and their families on their journey, which is unique to them and their loved ones. But as Covid crept into our lives and meeting in person became impossible, I felt inspired to create a story which could continue to support people with love and compassion.

As we entered lockdown, I welcomed Big Bear and Little Bear into my world. They, along with Doctor Bear, who I look forward to introducing to you later, identify with no particular gender, race or age as dementia does not care for these things. I created the characters in this way to ensure that this book is as inclusive as possible and that any lovely little bear could use this book to relate to their personal and unique situation.

I approached the fabulous illustrator, Iain Welch, with the concept and he brought the bears to life so beautifully. Creating the story of these wonderful bears injected such joy into some of the darkest days whilst working on the Covid wards so far from friends and family.

I would be thrilled if this book goes a small way towards building communities and generations of people who are kind, empathetic and understanding towards people and their loved ones who are living with dementia, and I do hope these lovely bears bring you as much comfort and joy as they brought to me and my inner child.

I think the important thing to remember is that your feelings are valid, and the loves, laughs and memories are always stored safely in a big bears heart.

Your Big Bear loves you just the same.

Big Bear and Little Bear are as close as close can be.

They love to nap and sing their songs, with Little Bear sat on Big Bear's knee.

Big Bear can no longer always do the things that big bears do.

Big Bear sometimes slows down and says,
'I'm not as quick as you!'

Big Bear cannot always remember who...

or what...

or where...?

Big Bear sometimes forgets these things and says, 'I'm a silly bear!'

Sometimes Big Bear forgets bigger things, things like Little Bear's name.

But no matter what Big Bear forgets, they love Little Bear all the same.

Little Bear could not understand Big Bear's forgetful head.

So Little Bear asked the Doctor Bear, and this is what they said.

'Big Bear has dementia, but Big Bear is still Big Bear.

When Big Bear forgets big things, like your name, it does not mean they do not care!'

Little Bear was confused by this, and began to feel quite mad.

Because when Big Bear forgets who Little Bear is, it makes Little Bear feel so sad.

Doctor Bear said they understood, and it is okay to not feel okay.

Doctor Bear explained Big Bear's dementia in a Little Bear friendly way.

'Our loves and laughs and memories are stored inside our brain,

like memory books on a bookshelf, to be read time and time again'.

'Our bookshelves fill from the bottom shelf up with everything we do.

The books must get stored higher as each shelf runs out of room'.

'So memory books on the top shelf store the things that you did last,

whilst books on the bottom shelf store loves and laughs and memories from the past'.

'But Big Bear has dementia, which makes Big Bear's bookshelf shake.

This keeps old memories at the bottom safe, but new ones at the top fall off and break!'

'This means Big Bear may struggle to remember the things you did today.

They may forget your name or age or games you like to play.'

'But because the books on the bottom stick to the shelf like glue,

Big Bear may remember things from being a Little Bear like you!'

'The fallen books are stored in Big Bears heart, they will always be safe in there.

Bears cannot read fallen memory books, but Big Bear is still Big Bear!'

'So, lovely Little Bear, whilst Big Bear may sometimes forget your name, the loves and laughs and memories are safe, and Big Bear loves you all the same.'

Little Bear ran home to Big Bear and gave Big Bear a big bear hug,

and was helped to make Big Bear's favourite drink in Big Bear's favourite mug.

They sang their songs,
then had a nap, with
Little Bear sat on Big
Bear's knee.

Little Bear now knew
dementia could never stop
them being as
close as close can be.

The end.

With a very special thank-you to my wonderful partner, Leon, and to my family, friends and colleagues who supported this idea and spent hours proofreading to help make Big Bear, Little Bear and Dementia a reality.

Dedicated to my Gran, Hilda.

Notes, thoughts and feelings

....

....

....

....

....

....

....